RESTING IN THE SHADE

Connect the dots from 1 to 10. Colour the p

1

1–25 Dot-to-Dots

©School Zone Publishing Company

BUNNIES' FAVOURITE TREAT

Connect the dots from 1 to 10. Colour the picture.

1–25 Dot-to-Dots

2

©School Zone Publishing Company

I LOVE MUD!

Connect the dots from **1** to **10**. Colour the picture.

3

HIGH IN THE SKY

Connect the dots from 1 to 10. Colour the picture.

4

SPRING HAS SPRUNG!

Connect the dots from **1** to **10**. Colour the picture.

5

SUPERSTAR!

Connect the dots from 1 to 10. Colour the picture.

TEN-GALLON TOPPER

Connect the dots from 1 to 10. Colour the picture.

OUT OF THIS WORLD!

Connect the dots from 1 to 10. Colour the picture.

8

1–25 Dot-to-Dots ©School Zone Publishing Company

TURTLE TOWN

Connect the dots from **1** to **10**. Colour the picture.

9

1–25 Dot-to-Dots

UNDER THE BIG TOP

Connect the dots from 1 to 10. Colour the picture.

10

1–25 Dot-to-Dots ©School Zone Publishing Company

WINDBLOWN

Connect the dots from 1 to 15. Colour the picture.

11

HOME-TWEET-HOME

Connect the dots from 1 to 15. Colour the picture.

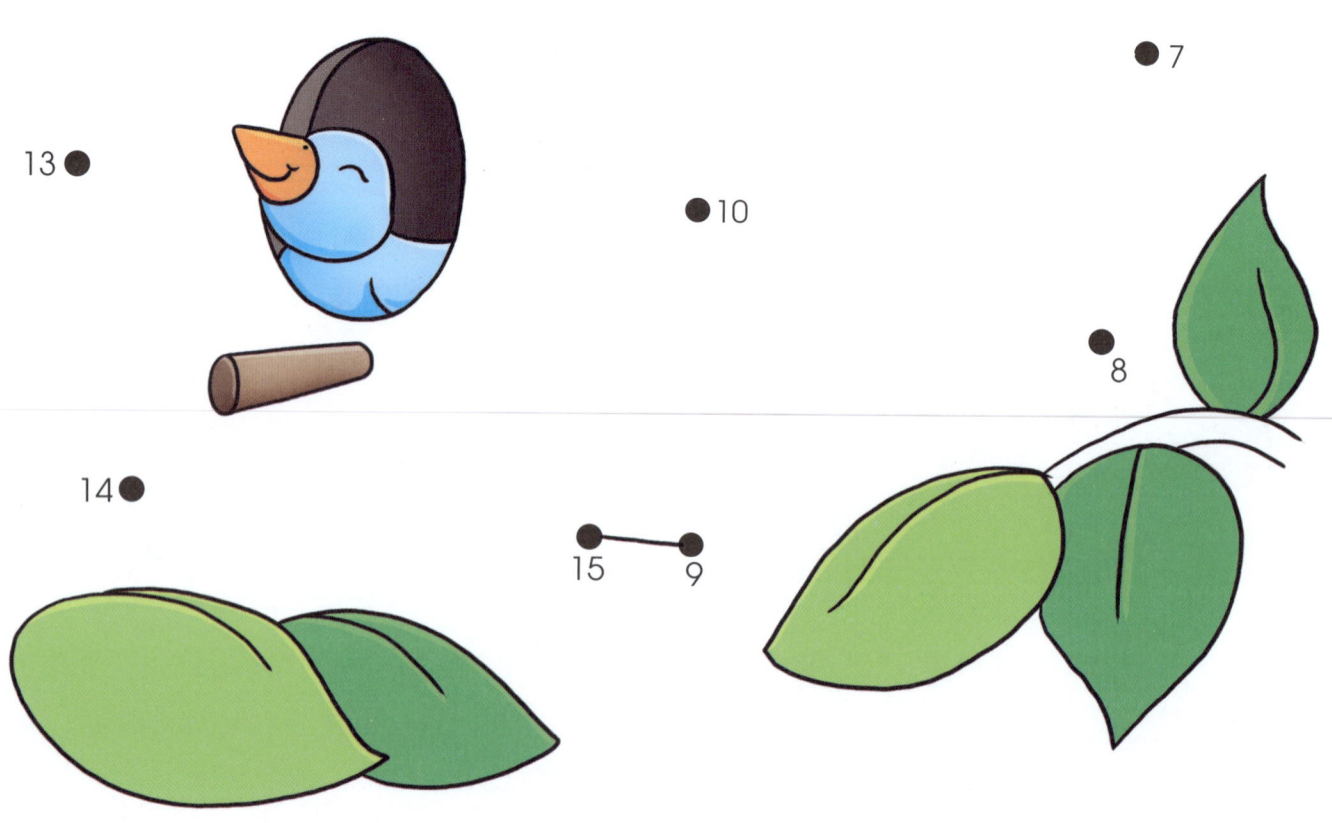

12

PUPPY LOVE

Connect the dots from 1 to 15. Colour the picture.

13

UNDER THE STARS

Connect the dots from **1** to **15**. Colour the picture.

14

BEDTIME FOR BUNNY!

Connect the dots from 1 to 15. Colour the picture.

15

POND PALS

Connect the dots from 1 to 15. Colour the picture.

16

1–25 Dot-to-Dots ©School Zone Publishing Company

SAY 'CHEESE'!

Connect the dots from 1 to 15. Colour the picture.

SAY 'CHEESE'! 17

SOMEONE'S CRABBY!

Connect the dots from 1 to 15. Colour the picture.

19

IT'S COLD OUTSIDE!

Connect the dots from 1 to 15. Colour the picture.

20

1–25 Dot-to-Dots ©School Zone Publishing Company

KARATE LESSON

Connect the dots from 1 to 20. Colour the picture.

21

FOREST FRIEND

Connect the dots from 1 to 20. Colour the picture.

22

GLIDING ALONG

Connect the dots from **1** to **20**. Colour the picture.

23

CUTE AND COLOURFUL

Connect the dots from 1 to 20. Colour the picture.

24

1-25 Dot-to-Dots © School Zone Publishing Company

AN EVENING CRUISE

Connect the dots from 1 to 20. Colour the picture.

25

HAVE YOU ANY WOOL?

Connect the dots from **1** to **20**. Colour the picture.

26

FLOATING ON AIR

Connect the dots from 1 to 20. Colour the picture.

27

OCEAN GIANT

Connect the dots from 1 to 20. Colour the picture.

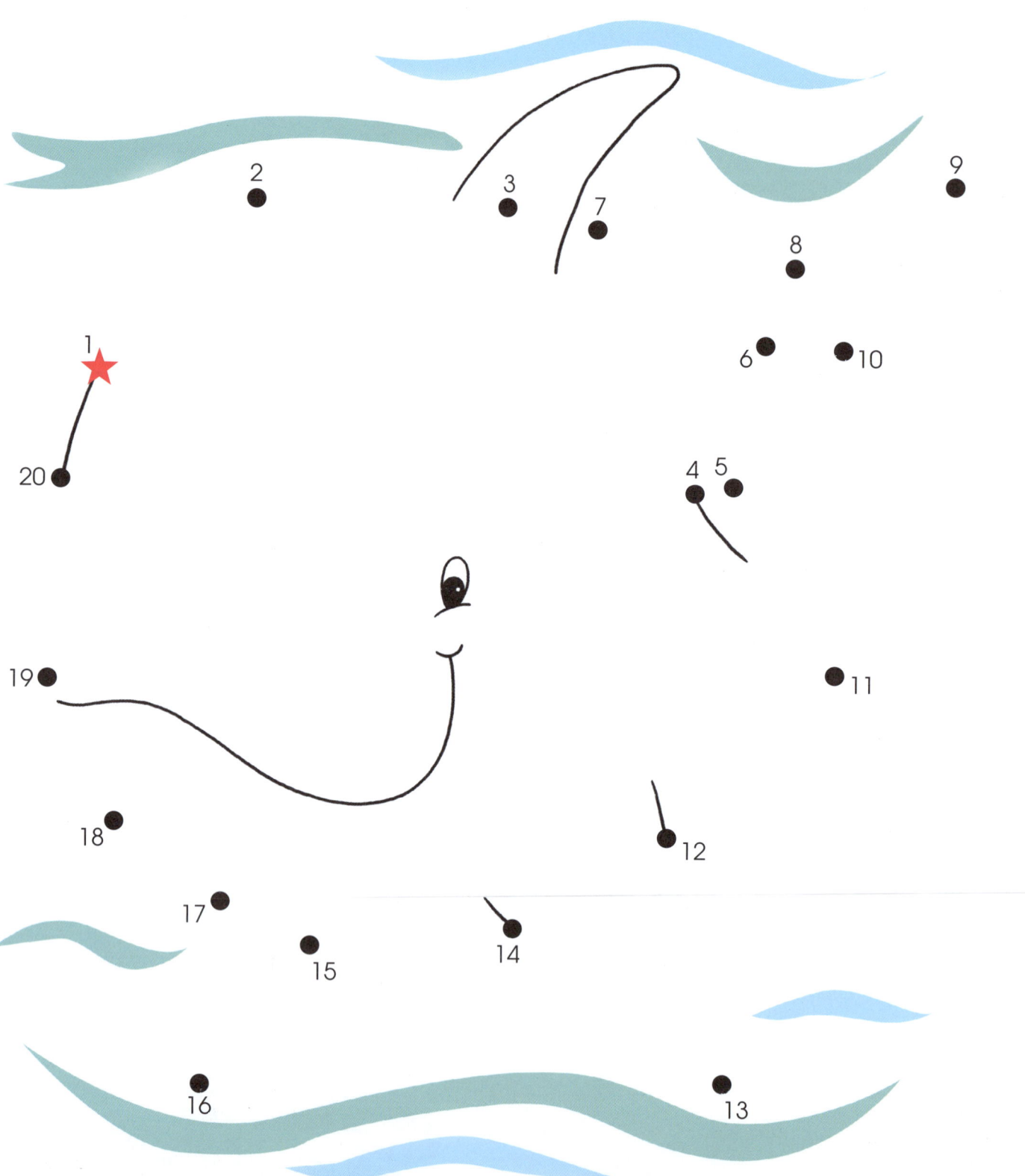

28

WOODLAND BUDDIES

Connect the dots from 1 to 20. Colour the picture.

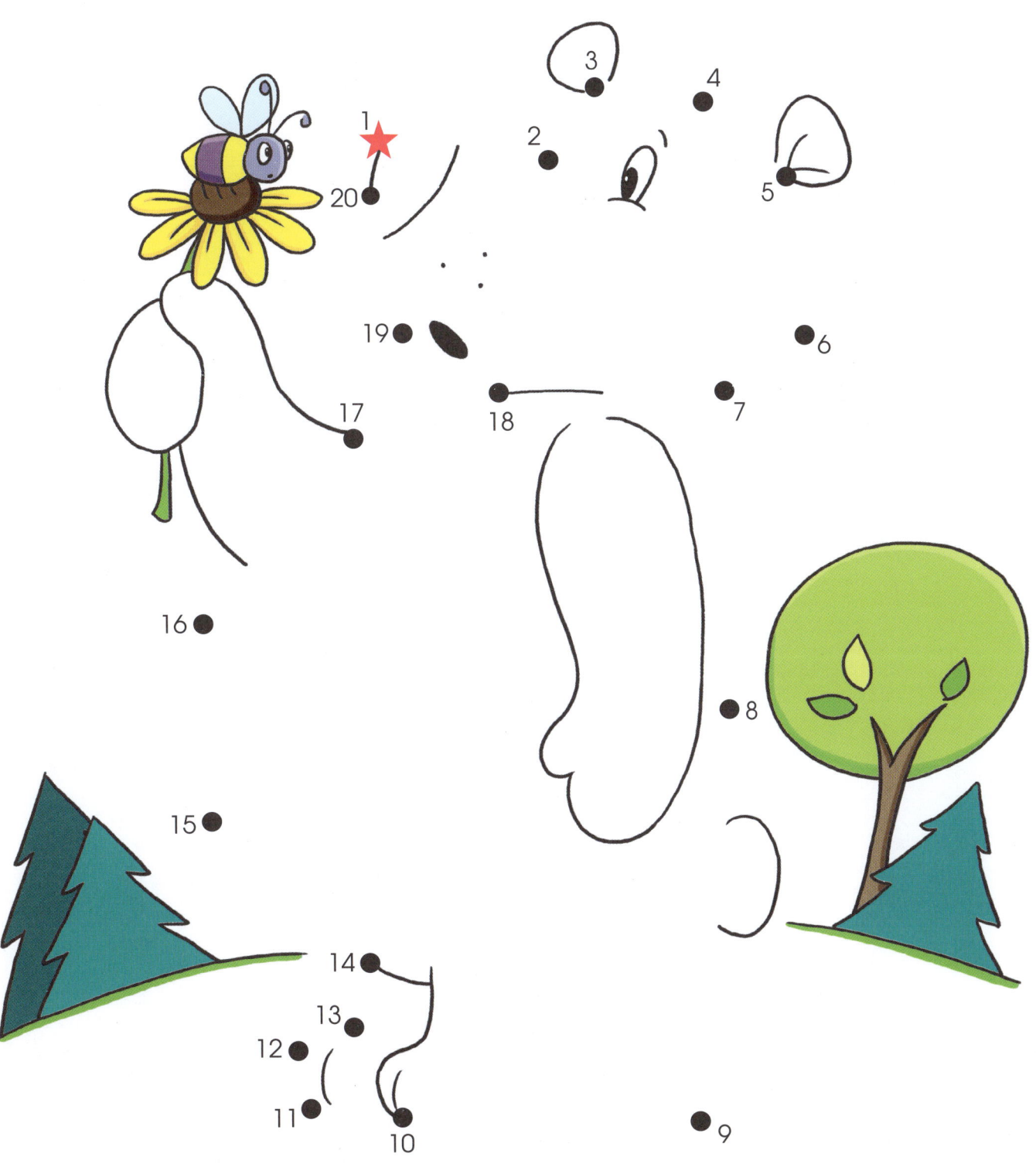

29

©School Zone Publishing Company

OUT TO SEA

Connect the dots from 1 to 20. Colour the picture.

30

GRAZING ON THE HILL

Connect the dots from 1 to 25. Colour the picture.

31

©School Zone Publishing Company

1–25 Dot-to-Dots

HORSING AROUND

Connect the dots from **1** to **25**. Colour the picture.

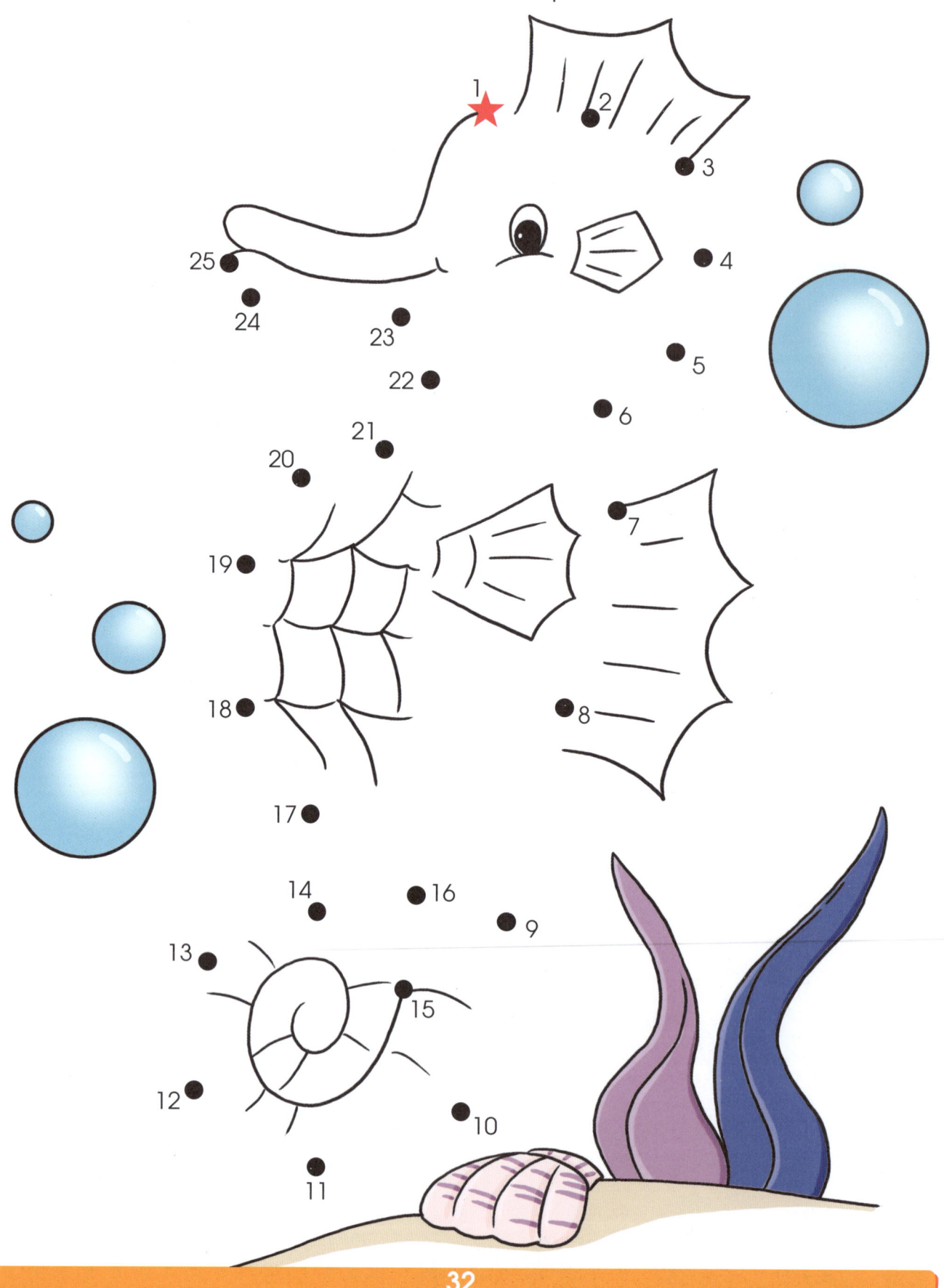

32

1–25 Dot-to-Dots ©School Zone Publishing Company

BLENDING IN

Connect the dots from 1 to 25. Colour the picture.

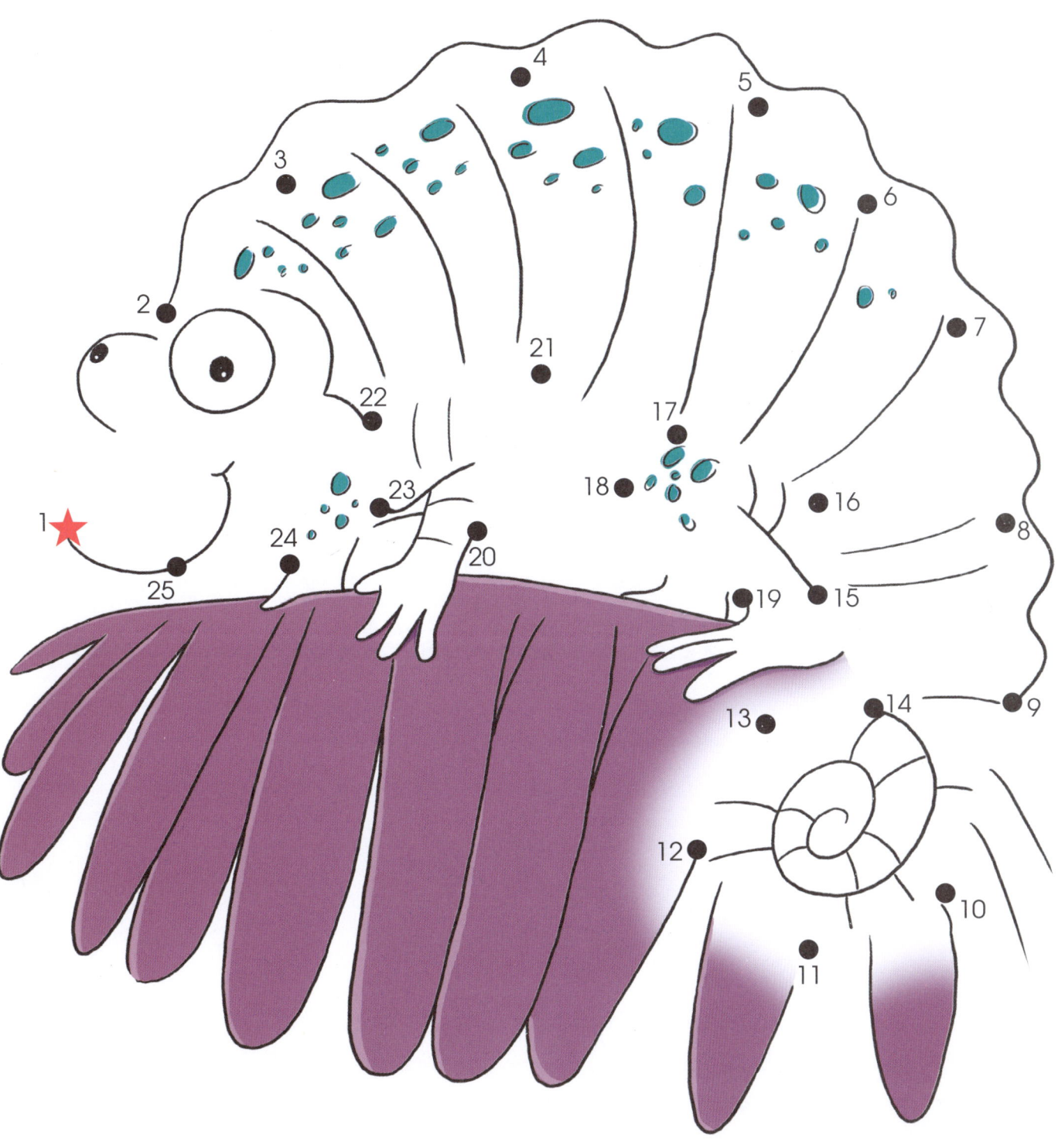

33

MAKE A WISH!

Connect the dots from 1 to 25. Colour the picture.

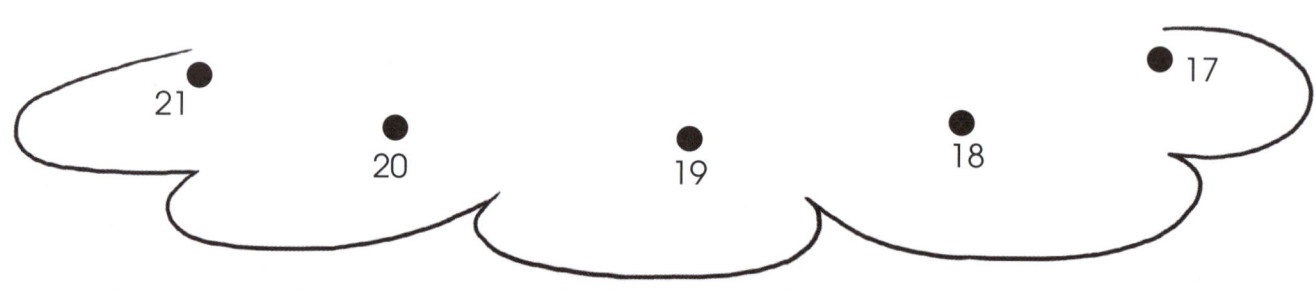

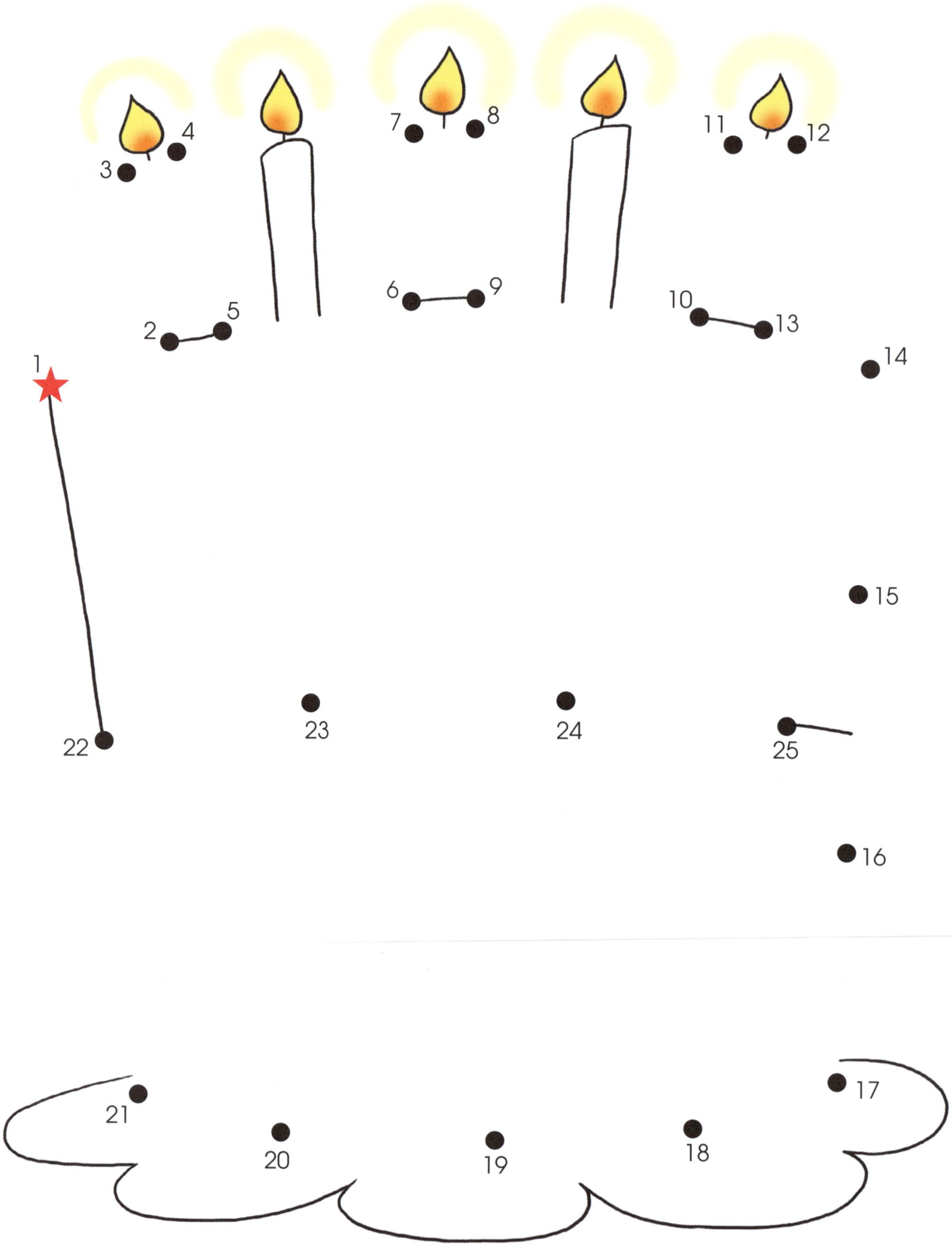

WHAT'S COOKING?

Connect the dots from **1** to **25**. Colour the picture.

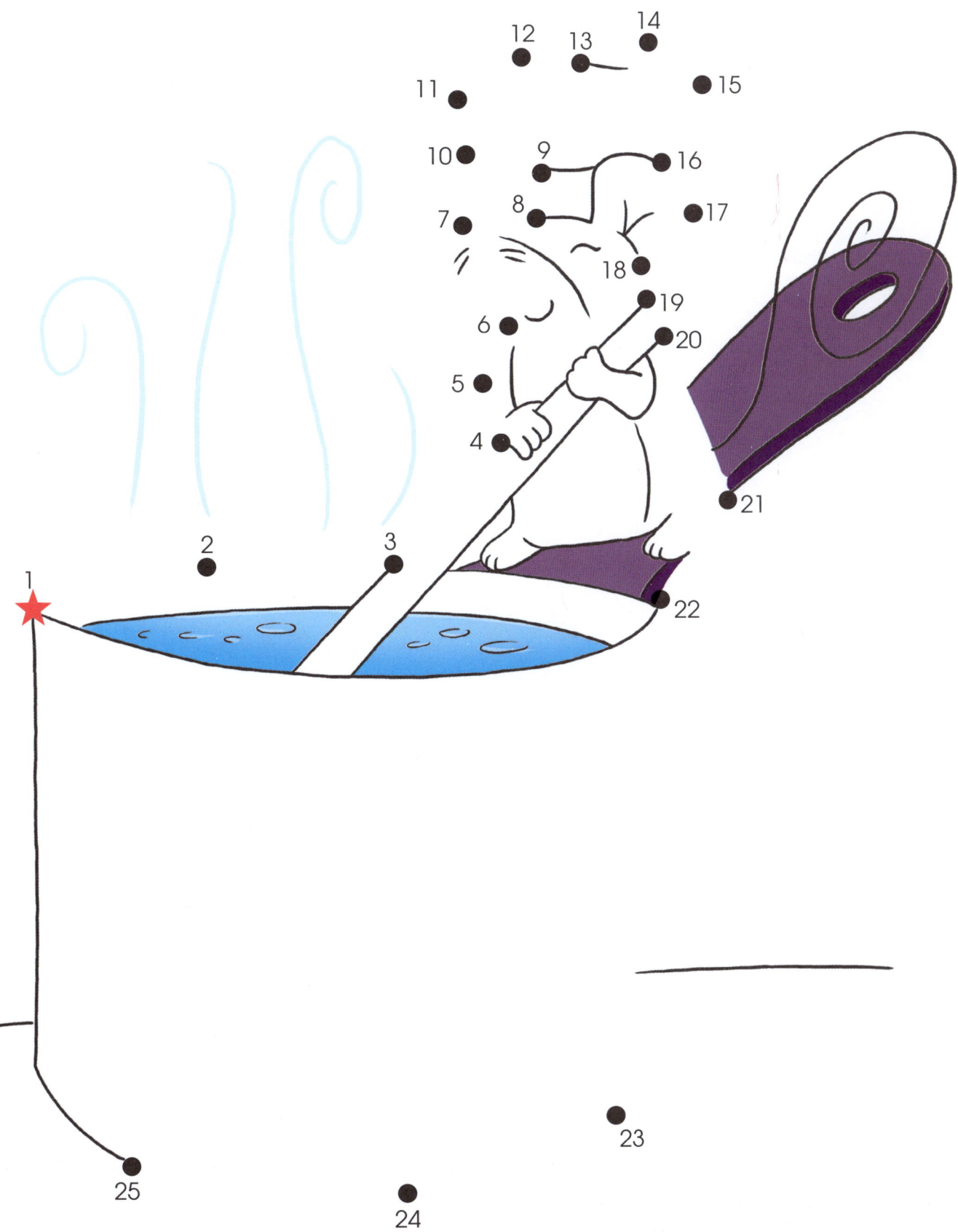

35

TOUGH GUY

Connect the dots from **1** to **25**. Colour the picture.

36

SWEET TREAT

Connect the dots from 1 to 25. Colour the picture.

37

TO THE RESCUE!

Connect the dots from 1 to 25. Colour the picture.

38

UP, UP AND AWAY!

Connect the dots from 1 to 25. Colour the picture.

WHITEWATER FUN

Connect the dots from 1 to 25. Colour the picture.

40

DESERT DWELLER

Connect the dots from 1 to 25. Colour the picture.

41

LOST IN A GOOD BOOK

Connect the dots from **1** to **25**. Colour the picture.

42

YOO-HOO KANGAROO!

Connect the dots from 1 to 25. Colour the picture.

43

DIVING FOR TREASURE

Connect the dots from **1** to **25**. Colour the picture.

44

PRACTICE MAKES PERFECT!

Connect the dots from **1** to **25**. Colour the picture.

45

OUT ON A LIMB

Connect the dots from 1 to 25. Colour the picture.

46

1–25 Dot-to-Dots ©School Zone Publishing Company

DON'T LET GO!

Connect the dots from 1 to 25. Colour the picture.

47

OCEAN EXPLORER

Connect the dots from 1 to 25. Colour the picture.

48

1–25 Dot-to-Dots

©School Zone Publishing Company

CHATTERBOX

Connect the dots from **1** to **25**. Colour the picture.

49

©School Zone Publishing Company

1–25 Dot-to-Dots

GOING FISHING

Connect the dots from 1 to 25. Colour the picture.

50

WHAT A HOOT!

Connect the dots from 1 to 25. Colour the picture.

51

HAPPY TRAILS!

Connect the dots from 1 to 25. Colour the picture.

52

A LITTLE BIT COUNTRY

Connect the dots from 1 to 25. Colour the picture.

53

©School Zone Publishing Company

NIGHT-TIME FLYER

Connect the dots from **1** to **25**. Colour the picture.

54

BEST BUDDIES

Connect the dots from 1 to 25. Colour the picture.

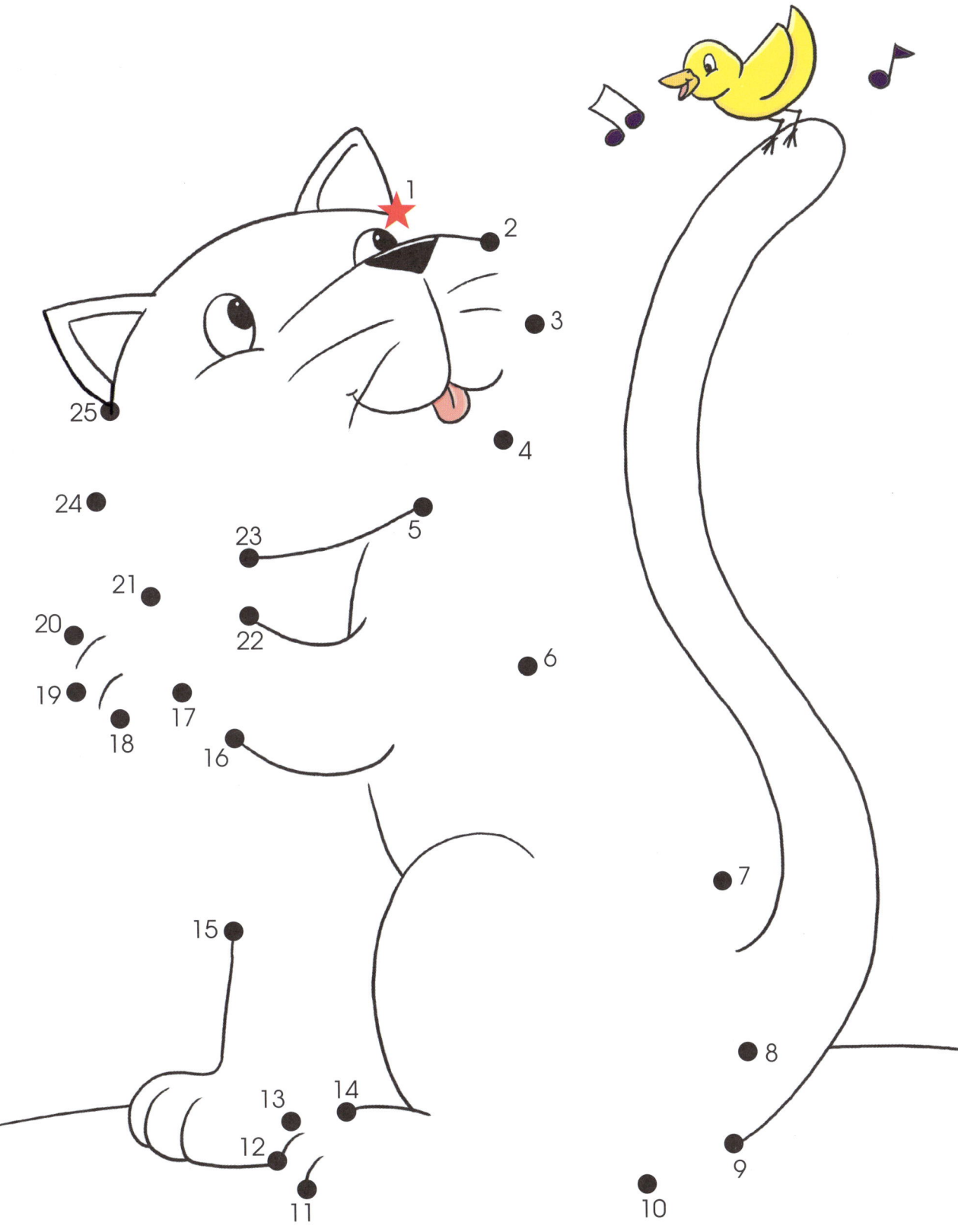

55

©School Zone Publishing Company

1–25 Dot-to-Dots

RACE TO THE FINISH

Connect the dots from 1 to 25. Colour the picture.

56

OUT ON THE ICE

Connect the dots from 1 to 25. Colour the picture.

57

IT'S TIME FOR THE SHOW!

Connect the dots from **1** to **25**. Colour the picture.

58

MIGHTY ROAR

Connect the dots from 1 to 25. Colour the picture.

59

DINO-MITE!

Connect the dots from 1 to 25. Colour the picture.

60

1–25 Dot-to-Dots ©School Zone Publishing Company

UNDER THE SEA

Connect the dots from **1** to **25**. Colour the picture.

61

BIRD'S-EYE VIEW

Connect the dots from 1 to 25. Colour the picture.

62

ROUND 'EM UP!

Connect the dots from 1 to 25. Colour the picture.

63

BATTER UP!

Connect the dots from 1 to 25. Colour the picture.

64